The Whole Existential Novel

The Journey from
the Dark Side of the Rainbow
to Satchidananda

POETRY

By Dane Ince

PUBLISH

EYEPUBLISHEWE
PUBLISHING POETRY, LITERATURE, ART, MUSIC
FOR HUMANITY'S SAKE
A BRAND NEW PUBLISHING COMPANY
SAN FRANCISCO
2020

ISBN: 979-8-9870259-0-1

Dane Ince

TABLE OF CONTENTS

Table of Contents

Table of Contents

Lagoon of Sorrows

On this day in the year of the horse
By the Lagoon of Sorrows
My hand touched this page of paper now
To leave behind a testament
A record, an artifact
A rose pressed between the pages of the book of our lives
Witness born herein that love was found
Cherished
Held close
The spray of waterfall water mist tasted
Refracted rainbow hologram
Waterfall dance of joy dance
Danced the dance of waterfall water joy
In a beating of my heart the river flows
Tsunami through my veins
This is the vow spoken by one man, all men me
The angel's benediction falls down
Mists kiss the face of one man, all men me
I speak this vow to my water fall angel
One word next to another word
A painter's brushstroke
Till finally we travel south
Searching for a better vantage point
The captain's map plots out a course
Around the island to the east
Where thunder is heard miles out at sea
Thunder from the beast
Spilling into the ocean from a time when lava had just
cooled
This freshwater waterfall sings
Sings out a poem
A poem from the heart
A poem along the shore
A poem at the edge of the lagoon

Dane Ince

Between the splash of sorrow
And the retreating moon
Hooves glide across the surface
Like a prophet on the Galilee
Mane and tail fly like winter storm clouds
Summer skywriter writing I love you
Big arrow through the heart
Finally floating away in memory
On this day in the year of the horse
By the Lagoon of Sorrows
I offer you this gift
This token
This gesture
This pebble in the sea
I love you Angel
I love you waterfall
You are life to me

Tears

Each tear snowflake like
Icicle drips rolling down
Homeward ocean bound

Dane Ince

Personal Ad

Man seeking Woman -49
Summer Sunday 17 years ago the search for love ended
It is difficult to ruffle your attractive plumage at a keyboard
Somehow typing ka-kaw ka-kaw,
I don't think is gonna get it
How about this
 I am howling at the moon just now
Can you hear me?
I want what the ocean wants before the ocean KNOWS
what it wants.
Sometime later She made it known that she had no idea
what the personal ad was all about and that she responded
because the age was right for her
Later that same day in response to her response
The poem starts out something like that- 49
I do not have an answer for the motion
Instinct
Quest search for the other half
To create a history that is bound up for eternity
To change the way things might have been
To watch something grow to maturity till it is tired and no
longer needs me to watch
I was there and you were there and we were there and we
were witnesses
And we can leave now

When the trial is over and the jury has offered up their
conviction and this dance
I think the poem starts out something like that and writes
itself in our waltz
In our minds
And on our bodies
Keeping time to the roll of the wave crashing on the sand
And baby boys play with sticks
And sisters kiss knees scraped on bricks
I want to finish this, but I am looking for another word or
punctuation to fill…
The music ended
The story ended tragically ever after
Howling now gripped in grief's strangling grasp
A song as old as planets dance across the sky
Waterfalls and snow
The medicine man's bitter herbs
Crow and Coyote laugh
Move old man move
The ocean in the seashell sings
Move old man move
Follow the jackrabbit
Follow the Buffalo
The search for love begins begins begins anew

Dane Ince

Call a cab

I have had that drug twice Propofol
You drove me home safe
Next time
Soon
 I will have to call a cab
It must be what death is like
Subsides terror pain after
The retreat
Of the lowest neep tide
I saw you struggle
I saw you die
When your heart stopped
I just stood in the corner
Watching the flat line
 I could not kiss you
Kiss you one kiss never enough
All the tubes and masks barricades
I could not kiss while you were still
Still able to know I love you
I tried to pack you up a sack lunch for the boat ride
I brought Callie and she stayed in her carrier most of the day
You did get to pet her
I was afraid
Scared you would know
Know this is the end
Goodbye
We trade notes on paper
Till your writing was unintelligible scribble
I asked if you wanted morphine
You shook your head no
 Are ready to go I asked

A little shake of your head no
Fiery eyes said fucking hell no
We looked at our wedding album
You pointed out the picture you like most
There are clever words for what it means to be afraid of
being alone
 The rustling whisper of wind through leafy trees
The smell of air just after rain
There is even a clever word for the absence of pain,
absence of sorrow
But what is the word for the sound that starts at my feet
Travels up through my belly
My vibrating throat
And out to the room where our cats sleep
There is no word only the sound
Today is a good day to cry
There is no clever twist coming here to finish this off neat
There is only the word
Grief

Dane Ince

Wintersong

Winter time waits Till all green gone
Steeple top touches Cold gray fog
Willow hems kissing Touching
Silent kisses Silent in
the mourning of Whispers fall
From tall treetops Doves walk on
Broken sidewalks Aching loss
Ringing out Sunday morning
Albatross Knowing this is hell
Like memory blisters on
My frozen feet Dirty
 Go back to sleep Roll over
To forget this nightmare dream
Ferry ride across the bay
Teardrops sway The fading day
sunset hugs the crying night
 On the hotel veranda
Teardrops sway just falling down
Tomorrow is
Tomorrow is
Another day

Drunk

She was a drunk
I loved her
She died
The cats she left behind
Have no idea where she is gone
When she is coming back
If she is coming back
Neither do I
And I saw her go
Turn pro now give up the amateur drinking
But I won't
I am too chicken
It is not a good look
The wasting yellow you turn
When your liver says fuck
I'm done
She looked like Pre-Raphaelite dream
Except for the color gaping mouth hung open
Just won't stay closed
I asked the nurse to take a picture
Of me holding Karen's face
Holding her mouth closed
You do not want that memory, the nurse tried to evade
Oh yes yes I do please take this picture
Of my large hands holding the seemingly small face of love
Of my last I love you
On her Raymond Chandler long goodbye

Dane Ince

<u>All on me</u>

Peaches, I am crying
This sorry ass confession
Sure, I am crying
There is no laughing
Good laughing to come after
Unless there is crying
It is not a condo for sale sign
Empty two car garage included
It's the am who am I
It is a single facet
That life fashions from me
Diamonds are just rocks
They cannot not sparkle
Without the grinding many cuts
Placed all about their bodies precisely
Just so
How we love the things that twinkle
Stars in heaven
Rings on fingers
If I were a poet
I'd just lie to you
But dear, I am just bleeding
Because that is what blood does
Bleeds and clots and bleeds again
Till it never stops
 But for that one last clot
The joke is all on me

Dung

In the beginning
Coyote ate a dung bug
That bug rolled him
This lesson is yet learned
Rolling down the mountain still
I speak to you from San Francisco
Formerly the lands of the Ohlone where they
Spoke Ramaytush
The language of the people from the west
Today on fentanyl dusty streets
A sad ballad of lost characters
Who imagine they are real
Dreaming to trade fantasy for the pain
Of blood pumping until it no longer does
"The spirits of ancestors roam everywhere", declares
Connects with Streetcars.
Sells Poems for money, a man, did not listen to the
proclamation. He never listened.
Never Stops Talking is shaking her head and bringing her
hand to her forehead
With her finger shaped in an L.
Connects with Streetcars rolls his eyes and just keeps to the
task of rolling his cigarette.
Members unborn to a tribe
By the convenience of society
They gather
Scattered encampments by the Lagoon of Sorrows
Crying I cry now
Hurtful hateful boiling flow
River tears weeping
Laughing coyote and crow
Trick us again, ending all

Dane Ince

Killing death murder
Of crows laugh and play tricking
Coyote me, slow
Slow to get the joke on me
Lonely blackness all in fun

Every day

Every day of the year someone dies
Every single time it is horrible
The ones left here
Are?
Fill in the blank
The time is always perfect no matter what you think about
it
Last time for everything comes
Numb and dumbly I stand there
She will never smile and laugh with me again
I know I am not alone but this island is so far away from
everything
But my grief
Bound together with all
Humbled
Little speck of sand
Glass comes from all the heat

Dane Ince

Ants

Every tube of paint I own is some fucked up shade of black
I grab a tube of alizarin crimson
Squeeze some black
Cadmium Yellow same deal
Even the titanium white is a very attractive
Glossy shiny b- l -a- c- k black
Midnight mineshaft roof ore collapse
I stab the canvas with a tube of cobalt blue
The rope of color oozes runs drips
The rainbow color wheel of blue black and gray
Adjacent color harmony
Hallelujah success
The pearls around the neck shine
The bright sparkle of raven eye black
Drink a beer eat a pastrami sandwich
Everything tastes just exactly like brick
Who can win
Puppy or 18 wheeler semi trailer truck
Who do you like
Sound good like the morning line favorite in the 8th at
Aqueduct
The mind plays
Tricks you with dull gray
Dumb dreams sappy
Sometime someplace long ago picture past
The kid Smiling with water wings on
Innocent
Swimming in an ocean of effluent misery
The family of open wounds goes on summer vacation

The travel trailer infested with worms ants and bitty bitety,
    spiders, scorpions, and ANTS!
The grand canyon boarded up closed
Out of luck
Haven't you ever seen a fucking hole?

Dane Ince

Liquorice candy

The last bag of liquorice candy sits here
Waiting wait waiting
Waiting for your return
Un opened Black black black
I howl you are never coming back
Tears boiling blood stain my face
I howl the howl of every man that lost
Lost lost lost their woman
Cast upon the sea of anguish
This boat of skin and bones is tossed
Till wretched and ill the soul vomits
Who likes liquorice dark
You do you do you do
And now you are gone
I howl like a poet all alone
I am sorry sorry sorry
Every word is vile and base
And feels so inept that only a scream and howl
Is more than empty
Empty empty empty
Take this candy with you when you go
If you will never come back
Do not look around
You will only see a pitiful me
Howling howling howling
Trapped in the pandemonium
Of this modern plague
A pandemic
Strangers meet
Here have some liquorice
It is dark and sweet
Something I will never eat
I am so sorry for your loss
We keep our distance as we meet

Paint Happy

I picked up a paint brush
Dipped it in a bucket
A bucket of blackest paint
When I touched the canvas
I painted moonless night
I tried to paint happy
But I cannot make my dead girl smile
If I keep drinking
Oh no worries I am not drinking
But the fentanyl fucking fine
Quoth the raven I want a shitload more
If I keep drinking
When I keep on keeping on
Will I ever see the rainbow there?

Dane Ince

Just another Thursday

During Covid 19
As in a dream
Recurring the slow motion chase ensued
Buzzsaw toothed clown chased me slowly
Paralyzed I could not move
Closer still I wake up
My wife died
Cats sat on my lap
Purring
I went to AA in Australia
I read poetry out loud in Berlin
I made art
I ate art
I listened to
Slack key guitar
Ravi Shankar
Tragic Tango
I ate a piece of David Bowie pie for comfort
I cried and cried and cried
All the dying beatings protest
A dark haired Russian ruined me with Tanka
I learned new language
Learned new words
I learned how to use pandemic in a sentence
I fucked my dead wife under a tree
I woke up from a nightmare to terror
Tragically ever after
A gift just for me
Having never left my office chair for this odyssey
I am grateful for the dimmer switch

Well Gus

I cannot scream howl crying all the days
From dawn till dusk
What about the future what are you thinking on Gus?
Starting over
Finding love
Hungry future- clowns just outside
The window of my shelter in place
Being given so many unwelcomed gifts
Spending all time unwrapping them
I cannot imagine doing that all alone
It is a losing battle I know
I shake my head
Wonder what was I gonna do
Wonder what I did
What I will do
If the story includes you
Smile whisper
Cry to me your joy
Your fear
I have nowhere to go
Except into you
And you into me
As old as the story is often told
One cup of lavender tea blossoms
A story for grandchildren yet to or never be
They dance this ancestor's dance
Coy and animal
So will you won't you
Lie next to me
I was searching where to lay down the book
The story of us
Not us and found many questions

Dane Ince

Nary an answer
Bent and broken
On the mend I am sure
I tell you I love you
Always have always will
Always always always
Where will we live in heaven
Where will we live on mars
A pas de duex we dance among the stars
Where will lyrics go
Where will I love you
Where will go lyrics
When lyrics go
Where will be lyrics
When lyrics will be
Dreams the heart
All I gift to thee

I did this instead

I forgot to go to my group grief session today
I wrote instead
I would love it if I could write every line as a volta
Open mic poetry reading from the imaginary,
Unwritten, unpublished work of Jack Lau Dromat
In the uncollected collection
"Ew. People, I only date unicorns"
I kissed a Unicorn in my sleep
Frolicking we were
On Florida panhandle beach
Under cherry candy clouds
Flowing mane like silk
Nearly invisible white
White as white sand
Bright as diamonds sparkle
A shiny sharp horn
Sliced my fucking guts out and I died

Dane Ince

<u>Despair</u>

I fucked despair
Rough, hard, long, fast
In despair's dark hairy smelly ass
One of the best fucks ever
The laughing kind
Laughing so hard you think
You both may not stop cumming EVER
And laughing you cum again
Crying out in ecstasy
Calling out to your favorite deity
We collapsed
Idiots grinning
Coffee stained yellow teeth
I smoke the last camel in the pack and again get hard
Rock hard
Cock standing straight up like a telephone pole
Just a pulsing under hot Arizona summer sun
Come here baby get some of this
Despair is my bitch

Habituated

I sent an out an unsolicited unwelcomed poem
It is a penance you pay for having a poet as a friend
They said
Take a shower and put on fresh clothes
Then take a long walk in fresh air
Was it cancer?
No booze
 BTW there is nothing
 To run away and hide from
What corner is safe
 Life is filled with pain
 I can write about it
Read it over and over
Some time later the stinger from the killer bee
Is removed
Habituated to my new life
Where the joy lives
With any luck and any love at all
I am becoming
Called by a name
Hoping to deserve it
The field of flowers on Misty Mountaintop
Nothing is prohibited everything is possible
 I am okay
Thanks for your comforting
I really love you for that
And for that I am grateful
What is the most comforting to me
Is the tea that I am brewing
Steeping forward trying
As best as I can
To be most fully
The who that I am

Dane Ince

Satchidananda

Where is the bus to Satchidananda
I borrow this for my own use
To put a word to what I am doing anyway
To let the sleepy part take a nap
So the rest of me can fully wake
I cut off my arms so long ago
Now I am reattaching them
"Sat" so my fingers can feel again that which is real really
Being, good, true, right, essence
I am seeing old things new
"Chid" consciousness
There is no place to go
When you are everywhere
I let the worry of dark alone
Settle to the bottom of the lake
I was always free
Just for the saying yes
Any place is holy land
Some are worshiped by you learning them so
"Ananda" Happiness, joy, bliss, seeing a fellow traveler on
dusty road
Sitting in the garden, talking, holding souls close, loving,
work
Existential Consciousness Bliss
Say hello and welcome to gentle, calm and kind
Till the release
Of the big let go

Toes know home

You found a bird's nest
You by asking
Opportunity placed at your disposal
Willingness to receive
Makes possible future present
No sorrow for chasing
Chasing what is chasing you
This is a lesson I have learned too
Forgetting forgetfulness awakes me to sleepy mindlessness
Not clear still pool perfect reflection of all that is possible
Any breeze flutter leaves makes
Snapping falling floating
Landing last upon the ground
Dirt they be now under feet
Feet chase chasing what is always chased
Stand still upon dampness
Confused
No place to bury toes as on sandy beach
Run on move on in wretched loathsome panic?
Fearing what might be
Blinded dumbly
To the gift that is
Ah fear my friend and I get drunk
I fight to crowd out this drunken song
Falling down is an easy win
For gravity is everywhere and never sleeps
Spinning it just spins
In stuporous vision I see you standing there
I lift my head from the barroom table
Drowsy between states of dreaming dreams
I see you not there
I lift my face now sober from the carpet of dead leaves

Dane Ince

Standing in bare feet on their dirt
Toes having no place to hide
Longing for summer sun painted beach sand warm
The lesson to learn is in standing still while we hurtle
through space
Over there is over here to someone else
So far is so close
A distance
A galaxy
Standing still
I have traveled from here to there and back again faster
than my blink
Waiting for the answer
Waiting to be caught
Chasing love is like chasing inspiration
I will remember how to let it catch me

Found

Tis but a dream dreamt
A tear's weeping wept
Truth, tenderness & forgiveness
Mutual respect
Consideration & warmth
Feminism art music & poetry
Curiosity labor unions & perennials
New England in fall.
Olive oil, bird feeders
& Dr. Bronner's toothpaste
The night sky
Unconditional love
I found this poem
I stole this poem and keep it handy in my heart

Poem Pictures

Unruly birthday hair smile
You at the start of a romance movie
Ready to ascend old wooden stairs
Proud of backyard homemade deep dish
Kayakers in the background bay of glamour sunglassed you
Roadside rocket gear woman
Queen surrounded by furbaby love sunny window smile
Sunlight park bench you have treats in the bag
Fountains bubble, I hear them
You fill the frame with interest against pink sunset clouds
Red wine ocean in a stemmed glass
The seashore worships before you
You are the beauty
You are the brunette
Watching whales in Mexico
These pictures ask me to ask to get to know you

I am a man

I am a man
The Fantasy is
On the platform of the Paris Metro
You ask me for a cigarette
Magically I have one
When I light it we look into each others eyes
Merci
Smiles
And I watch you smoke

<u>Soulmate</u>

A soulmate
Is like a sock missing its mate
You only find the missing sock mate
Once you have thrown away the solitary sock
Because you refuse to wear mismatched socks
Cold feet do not care
Nor do they know the difference

Sidewalk

Put the mouth in your mind
Around these words
Feel the taste of
The state
Beats
Women
In Portland
Remember the mouth feel
The bouquet
The after taste on tongue
Now swallow
Opus a day
Comes out not so easy
Frayed a little just around the edges
Anyone tired
Weary of no solution
Dumbly
Proud
Of the red, white, and blue
Black and blue
Beating!
Beating?
What kind of man
Is a man
Who thinks like that
Does like that
No man man
I tried to woo her
Every way possible
My attention just another assault
On her castle
On her perfect excuse

Dane Ince

To keep her loneliness company
All her very own empire
She dispensed its bounty
Without interference from any ruined man
Marlow, says," that's okay"
I am sorry
That it just did not land
Like butterfly on blossom
Really the arrow of Eros rips flesh
Wounds
Someday scars
Or always bleeds bloody pus
Type now solo sonatas
Stumble like a new dance old
Old dance new
Take it off
My coat off
Fold it like a pillow
Sleep on the sidewalk
Outside the fairytale
What is a bad man
Just a pattern for this man
While he dreams
On how not to be

Tu Te Amo

This is sick confusion
I love Spanish
Tu te amo
I write about trauma
Warning
It comes from life
This piece is untitled
All the words a spelled without any vowels
So it reads like growls and snarls
Like journalism
Ode to dying young and beautiful
As Poe preferred a proper subject for a poem
That's this one
And the next one
Flowers
Brush strokes
Moments
The shape of clouds
Before the dream I have every night
 I tell myself
In the dream
When things get tough
When the guy behind me
Won't leave me alone
I will look at my hands
Now am I in the hall
Where the lights are out
Duck and cover
Like that will work

Dane Ince

Lust of love bum

Crusty loaves of bread from the Arab market
Down the street
The last of the Kentucky Fried Chicken conveniently
packed packages
Of individual honey servings produced from the littered
coat pocket
Ripped open and spread right there on the gray curbside
Of the Rothko Paris dawn on the bared softness of a newly
born loaf
Vision from the corner of the eye
Crawls by special effects style
Tight black vinyl skirt
Legs atop very black spikey high high heels
Honey drops freeze in mid drop
Angel of lust floats wearily by
In an imitation pearl button sweater
Unbuttoned all the way down to downtown
Fluttering in her breeze
Breast bounce confined by a red bra
The honey drops from the edge of bread
And rolls down to the crotch
Of the pants of the grinning idiot on the curb
Orange sun slices through canyons of blue buildings
Honey flows

Thank you yes

Thank you yes
It is easy oh so easy to say no no no
I do it myself
I do it routinely
I do it everyday
No is safe
No is secure
No is unexamined
No is righteous
No is pure
No never won a bet
Never won a dare
Never got someone from here to there
No never passed a schoolgirl note from desk to desk
No is an action
No is reverse
It is completely understandable
It is completely within reason
I lose this battle everyday with myself
Do I say yes or do I say no
Thank you yes

Dane Ince

Months later

In the freezer
Open Hagen Das
Raspberry sorbet
Partially eaten
Plastic spoon rests there
Left eternally unfinished
As you have finished everything you could now
It was the last food I "made" for you
The first was caramel for strawberries
When I die the memory of your smile will be gone with me
But it is eternal in the minds of readers

<u>Peace</u>

All the possibility is right there
Just waiting like a path yearning to rise up and meet my feet
I wonder if I can see with new eyes?
Hear with new ears?
I want to heal not to fast nor to slow
Scaring the perfect scar just so
Hungry for hope
Knowing dark outcomes loom
And lurking right there ever present
An insult to the bright sun of tomorrow
I find peace

Dane Ince

Now look at what I let you make me do

Before the excitation of electrons dies down
I am pollinated by you
When you tell to get my shit together
It comes out in verse
Lost ancient rhyme
I hear you typing
Like colors sing
resonance like chanting resonates
Sympathetically collapsing like a vibrating bridge
Acceptance
I don't know you
And I wonder why when that will not be so
I suppose
Because everything is different
In this moment from the next
Everything changing everything
I can plant a flag there
But the wind blows
I am here to feel, see, learn, become, continue, to love, to
be free, to whisper, to whisper love things, love songs
proclamations, protest, to kiss the eyes of minds future to
what is now now now
Because one day it is gone gone gone
60's vibes and all
I stood there in the radio station bathroom
Looking out the window at a tree
Was the rainbow there
Was the tree there
Was I there
Thinking my LSD thoughts
Struggling to be more me than I might have courage for
To be okay with being

To make peace with myself
Explored examined categorized to my high satisfaction
I dug it
I dig it
I will dig it
I have been digging it all these many years since
If you dig this too
You are welcomed on the journey
I travel to the future Ramaytush
Clothed in the suit of my experience
I shed it at the beach
And swim in the cold pacific

<u>Because</u>

Because
Because I fell in love with a poet
Because I fell in love
Because I fell
Because I
Ok I drink by myself then
Okay I accept I die alone
The end
The beginning
 sorry I fell in love with you
I know you did not want me to
The fear that I would die
I would abandon you
Is more that you can bear
You claw at me to drive me Away
You win
this way
The way that you want it
I am weak and I fail
Everytime
I am ripped apart by the fantasy
That is not real
Because I fell in love with a poet
Because my wife
Died
Because I have three cats
Because I watch the sky
Because
Gravity
Because
I confess every imaginary
Once born
Alone

The Whole Existential Novel

Bloody
Yeah that makes me feel okie dokie
Yeah
I slept through sunshine
I understand
The mantle
Misty mountaintop
Straight jacket
Fingertip pokes my eye
Lie lie lie
I am grateful for the lie
The balm
Narcotic
Exhale sigh
purification
purgation
the absence of
 pity and fear
change
 results
confirming
the illusion
 in renewal
 restoration
This is not a meadow of flowers on a misty mountaintop.
This is midnight
 Disaster
I paint it
Hope that I capture
All
the ugly
All
the joy
Ce n'est pas une prairie de fleurs
Au sommet d'une montagne brumeuse.
C'est minuit. Catastrophe

Dane Ince

The solitary is not pitiful
But a truth
Sunshine is beautiful
Sunshine burns
Love is beautiful
Love is ugly
When I let you kill my soul
I am reborn
Because
Because
Because

Dance

Do you know the steps
Would you like to dance with me
The words cannot form out of my mouth
I fall down drinking punch
Junior high school punch
Humming bird feeder food
Blood red no 2 so you can see it when its gone
So you can miss it
It needs for you to miss it
Or you will not sleep
All night long
I will read vapid
Mindless today in Nashville
Hiding my private pain
old stale broken me
who needs a roadmap
just look me up
on the socials
hook me up
the stumble
me me me me
adjective me
intransitive me
pluperfect me
adverbial me
me me me
stupid sorrow singer
warm up
For the serving of cold guts
Teenage joke angst
Zombie dialect eludes
Do you want to dance
Hack poems phlegm

Dane Ince

The horrors
Quick step quick quick
Here comes the vomit truck
It is a secret dance called the stumble
Dance the falling tripping
Dance the blindness silent
Dance with empty shirt
Smell the faint fading loss
Shiver in the corner to the back beat beat down down beat
Shiver is the new step
It is all so exciting
The generation
Of useless
You cannot live without
Prime white gloved
Sepia snapshot
Gray dead you
Crazy
The dharma of broken things
That never mend
The dharna of sunshine
The dharma of misty mountaintop
The dharma of none of that
The dharma of the door
Yes one foot one foot
The other is a boot
The kicking busy
Stumble falling getting up falling falling
1 2 3 1 2 3
The wailing the wailing
The ruined wrecking
Waltz
It is a direction
Secret dance step
Impossible to dance
Yet simple by yourself
Just let it be falling

Satori Dolmen
The long time holding
The stumble is a dharma
My own stumble
All my own
Has its own dance steps
Do you know them too

Dane Ince

Why I can't move to a red state baby

They go sea of love
I go sea of misery
They go oh my pet toy poodle
I go oh my pet hyena
They go cuddle monkey
I go chimp ripped a woman's face off
They go tears of joy
I go crocodile tears
They go belly laughing
I go hacksaw stabbing
They go freedom liberty
I go fucking covid dead
They go botanical garden
I go fuck look a flower in the sidewalk crack
They look at the moon
I look in the mirror
They dance the fox trot
I dance junkie shiver and shake
They go fruit cocktail
I go peach from the tree
They say no to permaculture
I say no to culturally dead
Culturally dead is permanently dead, permadead
They say yeah Trump
I say I slammed the car door on my dick
They say honor and duty
I say when you fuck me just give a cigarette, I need to add
to my collection of burns
I say Black lives matter
They say all lives matter
Ah ah okay I'll give you that
Baby step on broken ankle logic
I say still Black lives matter don't you forget it
I wake up when I get up

The Whole Existential Novel

They wake up when they are dead
In "Cool Hand Luke" Strother Martin drawls the line
"What we got here is a failure to communicate"
What we got here is an epidemic that will kill us all dead

Dane Ince

I am not a poet

I am not a poet
I am a self important
Egotistical blabber mouth
It's all about me
I am addicted to telling you
In painful and indecipherably complicated detail
In obtuse adumbrated rhyme schemes abandoned in
ancient times, for good reason,
Every mundane scenario I lived through each day is if it is
important
As if as if it should mean something to you
The check out clerk cheated me out of correct change
My dog died
My lover ran off
Fuck you
Stab yourself in the heart
Bleed all over the page
Tell me about that
I just do not care
Someone is asleep
Someone fell asleep at the wheel
Missed the warning signs
Near miss running off the shoulder
No poems warn of the dangers of Alien dna
The first time I wrote this
I wrote no poems warn of the dangers of Alien jizz
But I am a coward and I changed it to fit in
I have been warned I have no right of provocation
In the arena of dirty talk nasty sex talk
I get it
I cannot be a bomb throwing provocateur
Like a woman or a gay man
So I scurry back across the Rubicon tail between legs
I am here now

On the dirt road detour in my two tone 1955 Bel Air Chevy
Pedal through the floor
Well-worn worries of sex with the devil
 Do fill up shelves upon shelves
Do not insert a lame poetic convention right here right now
When all you mean is a lot
Or more and more
Just say it simple clear
I am almost flying up with dust heading for the washed out
bridge
No streetlights
The Sci Fi Milkyway is splashed across the sky
Airborne like Themla and Lousie
Tell me a secret
 Only you know
Something that makes your hands shake
Trembly shading shaking You know
You know what I am talking about
Oh yes you do
Don't make me be graphic
Pornographic about it
To draw you out
Everybody wants it
Wants it dirty
Wants it sweaty sweet
We will all feel better
Collapsing into bed
Unless you would rather hear
Me talk about me
I can rock and roll you
All night long with that

Dane Ince

Shapeshifter

Periwinkle is my favorite tasting sound
Almost as nice as tango
Only not sensual, just raw sex
Like sad primates trapped in a zoo
Wrinkle the riddle of time upon your face I kiss and kiss
It makes me hard to see you smile
 Lukewarm bath water is tolerable after shots and shots and
shots
Mescal spilt on the couch what a funny joke
Mint grows wild all around this town
I must run away from mojitos all over the place
It is just some 1990's glitch
Just awful what they do to rum
What a waste I cannot take it anymore
No I won't
Is really what I mean
The hate burns incandescent in my chest
How will I escape this drunken madness
On foot on bicycle or airplanes?
Nope no way
I escape in my trusty "Shapeshifter"
Waiting and made ready there in the driveway
Rusty and dented no moss grows on it
It just rolls
My junkyard gem
Survivor of a Miami car crash in the fog
I was not drunk and driving at the time
It is just what I am told
Drip gasoline drop by tiny little drop
I ponder is it a little brook or stream?
Can I camouflage it with duct tape from the garage?
Cadillac Fleetwood Eldorado Seville maximum fins wills
Ragtop down rabid as I am

To get back to you safe and sober
Never sane when I think of you in your black camisole
"Shapeshifter" and I fly down the corridor
Between vineyards and ocean
 Sun and moon ninety degrees apart and setting
Seen from the Lost Hills Highway
I am just the messenger carrying the message of spirits
Written with the ancient planchette you keep in the pantry
The dream is your smile your embrace
While we watch straw colored mountains honeyed in
summer sunset

Dane Ince

Dirt Comes

It's like a volcano
Lava rolls down to the sea
Eventually cooling
Sea birds fly over
Sea birds shit on the cold lava flow
Rain Comes
Wind comes
Lava flow covered in a blanket
The seeds in the sea bird shit sprouts
And now we have pineapples
You however do not see all of this
All you see is the
Aluminum pizza pie pan slide across
Imitation wood grain Formica table top
Perfect slices of yellow very fake yellow
Pineapple glisten next to hot curled triangles of ham
In a lava flow of cheese.
Conjuring the spirit, the courage
To look into my soul and put down on paper
Note by note the symphony of freeway screech
Flower blossoms blossoming
The sound of stinky stuff not discussed
In polite company
To put one true word next to another
Like brush stroke on canvas
Like fingertips on thighs
Like firm hands squeezing
Drawing near
Looking deeply into the mystery
To see the mystery looking deeply back

The aristocrats hard sharp tongue flicks
Against the chambermaid's swollen loathing
Were the roles reversed?
There would not be doughnuts on Fridays
Afghan would still make you think of hairy stupid dogs

Dane Ince

<u>Voila</u>

I like poetry
No need for paints canvas
Or easel Just let the wounds bleed on paper
Voila Jackson Pollack

Light

Where we are wounded
Are the places where we can let the light enter
If we only open our shirts
To the sun and moon light

Dane Ince

Snuggle to awake

I am good like that completely stupid
What I know that scratches the itch
May be just be wrong for you
You see I just did what needs undoing
If I am lucky
 I can I can I can
Yes you can too
All need help
Some things are broken because everything is broken
Somethings me and you are broken all alone
All on our own
I did it to me
That what she said
Just before nothing
Just before gone
Makes me wonder what I am doing to me
The ocean is too big every day
Worst in a storm
I suggest running away
I suggest desert
Now that is where you can you can
Safest place to be
Stay away from the Hila monsters
And really do not keep Roscoe
The rattler
 As a pet
Were you with some one
Who Who has now gone away
Or is it pandemic
Or is it what you can't say
Just cannot think or feel
If you are inside or outside of the box
Looks like a sock puppet from where
Here

Fang, blood, and stink glands
All just for fun
All the voices of confusion should
Step out of that cavern
Lock up the gate
It is war to be sure
Filled up on fruit salad
Candlelight warmed
Chain mail
Head to toe
Safe in
Bubble bath armor
Makes ready for a battle with self
Knock down drag out barroom brawl
Get up
Get up from the startdust
Or lay there and bleed
What you need for healing
What you need to get better is for people to stop telling you
what you need to do to get better.
Witness
Hand
Look
Love
Touch
Psalms
All just there sleeping
Waiting for your snuggle to awake

Dane Ince

Hydra

Jar of hallmark jam always close
Finally technical break through yippie
On how to solve character names
Taking up too many syllables
Yeah me
Idiot
I do not know about me sometimes
As I contemplate birthday wishes for friends
"Don't Die yet fucker"
"Not on your birthday, don't you dare die"
Since my wife died no one laughs at my jokes
ITS A JOKE
She never did either really
Now I am suck in a loop
Fuck
I am stuck in a loop
She never really did either
Really she never did either
She really never did either
Really she never did also
Really she never did too
Really she never did to either or
None of that is true
Just not true lying poet chimes in
Nah really
That humor was glue

Bad Widow

I cannot say how much I love you
You are amazing
When you fall asleep after you touch your self
I sit here at 6 pm November
Dark surrounded by the empty
I wear a summer jacket of shots of mezcal
It is really just the blanket of the void
I pretend
I should win an academy award for principal performance
As a human
As a wreck
A crime scene
What is left after coastal hurricane
As disaster site
The flood
The toothless prostitution
Of extraction without novacaine
Do you know
The howl
The mark
When you see
Weak
You grab
Sorry
Clutching
Wishing
Begging
Fuck let me unlearn
What I know now
Whisper
For peace
A whimper
At the artifice

Dane Ince

Socially acceptable presentation
Of what passes for
Contemplated art
Serve me up
Silence
Leave me to the worst
Nothing can return
My stupid innocence
No click or smiles reach the island of me
Only bad widows have any answer at all

Avocado chant

What I did on my summer vacation
Woke up
Drank coffee
Watched CNN
Watched cats
Eat a banana
Wrote a Trump sketch
I made a fresh pot of coffee
Watched a comedy special
Entered my daily futile protest on twitter
On Facebook sent unwelcomed poems
Was invited to read on Sunday
Entered my futile daily protest on facebook
Replied to emails
Contemplated attachment thinking
I used to wonder
But now I have lived long enough
Through enough stuff
To know the answer
It is just me
No one is coming to the recuse
Contemplated mindfulness
My idea of it or theirs?
What is the purpose of skin
If it is not for touch
Just a bag
To hold the blood and guts in?
Listened to Tango music
Petted Cally as she demands
Replied to my late wife's sister thanking her for the flowers
Sobbed deeply fully completely loudly for as long as sobs
needed to be released
And for what seemed like forever
But was probably a minute and 12 seconds tops
Felt better

Dane Ince

Watched cats sleep
Watched cats snuggle
Watched cats go crazy over fresh birthday flowers for my
late Karen
Wondered what to have for breakfast
Grated Costco cheese to fill a gallon bag full
Just rewrote that last line
A blend cheddar gruyere, Bavarian emmentaler
Wondered if everything is dwelling in the past
Can I write a poem right now in this moment and still be
present?
Just re read this thing several times
Wondered why Microsoft word knows how to spell
Bavarian
But thinks emmentaler should be emmantled
Looked up emmantled
The word you've entered isn't in the dictionary.
Click on a spelling suggestion below or
try again using the search bar above.
No no trying just do
Thank you star wars
Automatic writing?
Get ready to read at a zoom event.
Think about reading at another zoom event
Looked up the word gestalt
Tango music playing cats sleeping
I sigh
I put on pants
Make bacon eat bacon
Think about pigs
It sucks to be a pig
Slice an avocado
In two
Remove the seed
Fill each half of the avocado with mild salsa
Eat the avocado
I wrote this just now

So I could see the word avocado in my mind
And repeat it again and again
It is an Avocado chant

Dane Ince

Good Garden

Before the flood on the river Styx
Burned everything to the ground
When I was sleeping on a bed of fresh hay
Before the dark day was bright as noon black
I never noticed
All the same
The before
The after
The beginning
The end
No line between
Sleeping
Waking
Painless
Joyless
For lack of appreciation
Of the dark side of the rainbow
Where I find myself lost
I see you shining
Out of my temporary cottage window
Beyond distant mountain
Forest pines
Whistle sing me out to play
Out of my dark house
Painted pain
Between Ultraviolet and infrared
Tip top dance on stars
This is a good garden
Grown by you

I can live here awhile
Knowing what I know now
Peace
You warm on my face
Sunshine wisdom
Bohdisatva Bohdisunshine

Dane Ince

Phosphenes

Perceived points of light
We are known by what we love
Starting with oneself
Shape of your lips
Places your mind travels
Songs of your heart
Line of sleeping lids
Speaking your dreams
Across the vibration
To gossamer satellite sing
Sting the tattoo
To pixel picture
When you sleep
In night light glow
Weave of fingers
Voice in protest
Voice in song
Whisper
Thank you
Widow's red rub eyes
Lamenting lost
Is that lost desert island
Left behind free
Carry lift of life
Secret scar star shines
Select sensation for the chosen
Lifted bed clothes invitation
I waited for
Now comes
Feels like liberation
Blanket warm nebula
Sound winter
Surrenders to the tender

Impression of love
Pressed upon the sparkle
Phenomenon without entering
Spray light the eye
Perception rays delight

Abracadabra

Form poems

Spoken word made real
Cyclone yesterday moon rise
As I speak create

Words disappear
Summer sunset into night
Magically here

As it was spoken
Like long ago moon lit night
Magic comes to pass

An amulet word
Winter malaria cure
Pure Starlight magic

Winter bends the tree
It comes to be as spoken
Spring holds the magic

Ever is

It is about the breaking
It is about the coming
It is about the finding
It is about what is the doing after
It is always about the journey
The journey that comes after
After everything is blinding
Stabbing darkness to everything and you
It is about
Who you meet on the road
The way you travel in this wildness of you
Sing to yourself loudly
You will be joined by a chorus
Of those who know broken
Hear them singing with you
You are always alone as everyone always is
One drop in the ocean
But the ocean
Is made from all the drops
All the drops all the drops and you together
All the drops that come crashing
Washing beach sand pure
As if nothing ever happened
But you were there
And I was there and we sang
Horror sadness and joy
In harmonic discord With
As wasps weak we were in our love for figs
We climbed inside and died
Now inside Rachel's six year old stomach
Now this is where we reside
Our babies flown out of host
In holy land as it was
Always holy and ever is

Dane Ince

Dark hand

This big dark hand grabs
Pulls me down
Won't let go
Blows in
Robbery from the past
 Steals the future
Deal with the dealt
Give up the ante
Go all in
Or go home
No in between
Only the right side or no side of you
You crown me
Empathy love
we go down to sea glass beach
California coast
You and me
Wander accidently to Big Sur
That window without any p a i n pane
The suffered
Etched pebble collection
To filled stained glass castles
Windows with enough
Sparkle of tomorrow's promise
I assure you
It is not enough
To stop the worry in your heart
You made the accusation
Then I joked did you do likewise
I know you did not
Wicked widow whispers
Slaughtered lamb language
Educated monks trade jokes
I am a sorry lad tattooed
Rust under carriage hidden

The Whole Existential Novel

Babble the clown tongue
On water spray flower
Plastic post it note
All the things ciphers cinders
Consider now used to be hopeless
There is a way to hold you holy
It is a practice
I relearn everyday
Grateful for the sway
Strength of branch
Supple tree lesson

Dane Ince

Protagonists

Everyday you hold me
Love me soft serve melting
Sticky hands and I do not care
Blew up my soul bag empty
Sparkles fly out the Scottish pipes
The emigration contemplation
Storm twist the bow into a neat holiday noodle
When you get to the end of the chapter
The plot twist leaves the protagonists
Bed clothes entangled
Sleep deprived
Red eye lust
More and more tomorrow
The promise finally comes
Stitches widow wounds
Into twin heartbeats
Bedside dimples spirits
Everybody runs out
Except the chosen
They know they never can
Always seeking home
Here their conviction
Never allows any option
Fire the browse back in
The challenge they meet
Full heart hands cup the baby sparrow
Flies off now not a blinking thanks
I do not think of dead spouses today

About <u>EYEPUBLISHEWE</u>

Eye publish ewe (EYEPUBLISHEWE) is a brand new publishing company, founded in San Francisco. Art, music, video, poetry, and other literature will find inclusive shelter here. Quality work produced by the artists' heart, mind, and soul rather than commercial interests will have this as a home. All are welcomed with open minds and hearts and eyes to the future. Together we will publish art for humanity's sake.

Founded during the pandemic of the 2020s, we have our eyes, ears, hearts, minds, and souls facing the future. Decades ago, the founder of EYEPUBLISHEWE pondered the ever-present questions of how the artist relates to audience. No answers were found then. Naturally, these questions are ones mired in all manner of human considerations. The making of money is the largest obstacle. But it ought not be the sole reason why an artist's quality work is kept from finding its audience. In the face of such events, all our lives are lessened. When this happens, it is a tragedy.
EYEPUBLISHEWE sees a world full of promise and possibilities where amazing artists who create wonderful content can find their audience. It is easy to blame the gatekeepers. We acknowledge they are there and move on to build our own counsel fire ring and invite new and not widely known storytellers to come out of the dark night shadows and share their lives with the world. Outsider art is mainstream now, if we imagine it so and yes, we can.

At a Mardi Gras in New Orleans in the days before
internet, a poet held up his xeroxed copy of his book of
poems waving it in the fresh air and singing out "Buy my
poems so I can sell them". The work of another poet,
much more famous locally, blowing bubbles in a bumble
bee colored cap on the sidewalks of Berkeley, California is
practically lost to the rest of the world.
Courage, vision, and the ability to say yes are what is
needed. We can, because we will, and we will do.

Yes we can
Si nosotras podemos
Si se puede
Ano, můžeme
Hai, dekimasu
はい、できます
Da putem
Is féidir linn
Ouinous nous pousons
Tak, ми можемо
יא מיר קענען
Ya mir kenen
Wi nou kapab
Tak możemy
हाँ हम कर सकते हैं
haan ham kar sakate hain
Hongu tinogona
我们可以
Wǒmen kěyǐ
Si possiamo
Ya kita boleh
Tha sinn a' cur
Bai, ahal dugu
Si podem

Yes, we can because we do not need to own a printing press anymore. With clicks of buttons and the flight of harnessed elections we can make art, music, poetry, literature, and all manner of our heart's desires available to the world in an instant. The ocean is just now curling up to form a tsunami wave of imagination and communication and we can ride it if we will just surf on it to sharing all that makes us human.

Just as the photographic camera changed the way painters painted, the computer has changed the potential for how all art forms are made and shared. EYEPUBLISHEWE, plans to be a part of the coming renaissance and hopes you will join in the creating and experiencing the art for humanity's sake that is available now or just coming into conscientiousness with each new day to dawn upon us.

EYEPUBLISHEWE envisions a future with traditional books, like court painters of portraits are still here, and a place for new formats for literature that employ words, sound and vision. www.eyepublishewe.com

About the author

The awakening began in a small grove of black oak trees on Collins Street in Fort Worth Texas. Then the road wound around a few stops in other towns and cities of Texas, Zapata, Del Rio, and finally ending with radio days in Space City. Under summer fog, the strong lure of Berkeley Dane Ince came west to study fine art and acting and to write ever so occasionally. Personal tragedy and the pandemic focused the artist's mind and hundreds of poems have resulted along with special online programing events on Facebook. "Outrage Against Racism" which was produced on the author's birthday and happens to land on Holocaust Remembrance Day followed by St. Valentine's Day Mascara an inclusive international and grown-up version of the celebration, Juneteenth was produced on the inaugural national holiday for the celebration of freed slaves in America, an international Day of the Dead event, and most recently, an event being a poetic gathering of writers from around the world in support of Ukraine. Dane Ince is an internationally published poet, named Beat Poet Laureate for California, and hosts a weekly open mic- Time to Arrive, and founder of EYEPUBLISHEWE.

Dedication

To my wife Tish

Life is a good mess to be in
You were laughing in your dream
You woke up angry
The mind mistake is to think
One thing is just one thing
Pure
Like bliss
This
Illusion
Confusion
Persists
One thing is nothing
One thing is everything
This too traps us in the box
Perception
Wanting what we want
Love
Affirmation
The call of your name
Within the earshot of all in town
I worried about all the wrong things
Love is love
I wondered how to finish this
To make the bow just right
Gleaming wrapping paper
The tapping time shuffles
Falls silent
In my one clear voice
I say
I hand you my heart
You are my best and only lover
I am so desperate for this nightmare pandemic
To fall asleep and dream better dreams
Where everyone knows
That you and I
 are we
I love you Tish

Dane Ince

www.ingramcontent.com/pod-product-compliance
Lightning Source LLC
Chambersburg PA
CBHW022105020426
42335CB00012B/836